WHY WE GET WORRIED

A Practical Guide to Letting Go of Worry and Anxiety and Living A Stress-Free Life

Jose Andrews

Why we get worried

Disclaimer

The advice and strategies in this book are provided for general informational purposes only and are not intended as a substitute for professional advice. The author and publisher disclaim any liability for the decisions you make based on the information provided.

Why we get worried

About the Author

 Jose Andrews is not just an author but a compassionate high school counselor dedicated to supporting students and parents in navigating the complexities of stress and anxiety. With a wealth of experience in the educational field, Jose goes beyond textbooks, offering practical guidance to foster resilience and well-being.

Beyond the counseling office, Jose also loves the world of music. He plays the piano and violin not just as pastimes but a harmonious expression of his creative spirit. The transformative power of music fuels his approach to life's challenges, emphasizing the importance of finding your unique rhythm amid the symphony of daily struggles.

What sets Jose apart is his genuine desire to help people conquer their fears and worries. Whether it's through the written word or one-on-one counseling sessions, Jose's commitment to making a positive impact shines through. His insightful guidance extends beyond the academic realm, reaching into the hearts of those seeking solace in the face of anxiety.

As you journey through the pages of "Why We Get Worried," remember that the wisdom shared by Jose Andrews is not just rooted in professional expertise but enriched by a sincere desire to make a difference. In both his counseling endeavors and his literary pursuits, Jose continues to inspire and uplift those in need.

Contents

Introduction

Our journey through life is like a rollercoaster, filled with thrilling highs and challenging lows. Yet, what sets the course for our future is not the ride itself but how we navigate its twists and turns. Picture life as a grand puzzle; the pieces may not always fit perfectly, but it's our choices that determine the overall picture. In the pages of this book, I invite you to explore strategies that not only help you weather the storms but empower you to thrive in the midst of uncertainties.

Worry and anxiety, like unwelcome hitchhikers, often sneak into our lives, adding unnecessary weight to the challenges we already face. They are not problem solvers; rather, they masquerade as solutions, burdening us with extra baggage.

The question then becomes: how do you steer your ship when the waves of worry and anxiety threaten to rock it?

How do you shed the load of worry and anxiety?

How do you resist the temptation to carry these additional burdens, so that you can channel your energy toward tasks that truly matter and cultivate a life filled with genuine happiness?

I have done my best to strip this book of all the regular jargons you'll usually find in a book like this. All there's left is simple, actionable steps. Whether you're a seasoned explorer of the self-help realm or taking your first steps, the insights within these pages are crafted to be accessible to everyone. I've aimed to make the journey toward stress-free living an enjoyable stroll rather than an arduous climb.

Think of this book as a friendly companion, offering a guiding hand as we embark on a walk through the landscape of stress management. We'll navigate the winding paths together, discovering not only how to weather the storms but also how to dance in the rain.

For those hungry for more, additional resources await in Appendix II—an opportunity to delve deeper into the vast realm of stress and anxiety management. Consider it a treasure trove, ready to be explored whenever you feel the need for further guidance.

So, my friend, let's take a walk—a walk through the pages of this book, a walk toward a life where worry and anxiety take a back seat, allowing the vibrant hues of joy and fulfillment to paint the canvas of your existence. The journey awaits, and I'm thrilled to have you by my side.

Are you ready to stride toward a stress-free, joy-filled life? Lace up your metaphorical walking shoes, and let's begin this transformative adventure together.

Why we get worried

Chapter 1: Understanding Anxiety

The Nature of Anxiety

In our everyday lives, stress often becomes an unwelcome companion. We've all experienced it – that tightening in the stomach, the relentless thoughts, the ever-present hum of unease that seems to linger in our minds.

Welcome to the realm of anxiety…

If we could just take a moment to carefully look at this complex emotion, we'll discover anxiety isn't just a buzzword. It's a response wired into our biology, a survival mechanism that once served our ancestors well. Picture this: you're in the wild, facing potential dangers like hungry predators. Your body gears up, heart pounding, senses heightened – that's the fight-or-flight response, the core of anxiety.

At its core, anxiety is a physiological and psychological response to perceived threats. Our brains, wired to protect us, activate a cascade of responses to prepare for danger. This includes increased heart rate, heightened senses, and a flood of stress hormones like cortisol. In the wild, these reactions were vital for survival, ensuring our ancestors could respond swiftly to predators.

Fast forward to the modern age, and our stressors have evolved. Bills, work pressure, social expectations – the predators may have changed, but the body's response hasn't quite caught up. We find ourselves equipped with a survival system designed for the wilderness in a modern world, and that doesn't quite serve us right

Understanding anxiety is the first step in your journey to an anxiety-free life. It's not about eliminating stress entirely – that's neither possible nor desirable. Instead, it's about recognizing when our ancient survival instincts are working overtime, causing more harm than good.

Distinguishing Healthy Stress from Chronic Anxiety

Stress, in its essence, isn't the villain. It's a natural response that keeps us alert and motivated. The adrenaline rush before a presentation or the heightened focus during a deadline – these are manifestations of healthy stress. It's when stress becomes chronic, unrelenting, and disrupts our daily lives that it transforms into anxiety.

Differentiating between the two is pivotal. Healthy stress propels us forward, urging us to meet challenges. Anxiety, on the other hand, often paralyzes, preventing us from functioning optimally. The first step in conquering anxiety is recognizing when stress transitions from a motivator to a formidable adversary.

When Anxiety Becomes Chronic

Without control, anxiety becomes chronic in nature. We know it has become chronic when it begins to infiltrate every aspect of our lives. Chronic anxiety can manifest in various forms – generalized anxiety disorder, social anxiety, panic disorder, among others. Each carries its own set of challenges, yet they share a common thread: an overwhelming sense of unease that extends beyond specific situations.

The impact of chronic anxiety isn't confined to the mind. Mental health is intricately connected to our overall well-being, and unmanaged anxiety can manifest in a myriad of physical ailments. Prolonged exposure to stress hormones can contribute to cardiovascular issues, weakened immune systems, and digestive problems.

These begin to take immense tolls on our daily lives. Relationships may strain, work performance may suffer, and the simple joys of life may be overshadowed by a persistent sense of unease. It's a cycle that feeds on itself – anxiety begets stress, stress begets more anxiety, creating a loop that's challenging to escape.

The First Steps to Overcoming Chronic Anxiety

You are not alone in this

Before we delve into the strategies and techniques for an anxiety detox, it's crucial to address the stigma surrounding mental health. Anxiety is not a sign of weakness, nor is it something one can merely "snap out of." It's a real, complex condition that requires understanding, compassion, and effective coping mechanisms.

According to the Anxiety and Depression Association of America (ADAA), anxiety disorders are the most common mental illness in the U.S., affecting 40 million adults. This means that statistically, someone you know – a friend, a family member, a colleague – has faced or is facing the challenges of anxiety.

So you are not alone. Everyone, at some point, faces the challenges of anxiety, and seeking help is a courageous step towards a healthier, more balanced life. It's not a sign of weakness; it's a testament to one's resilience in navigating the complexities of the mind.

Becoming Aware

The journey towards an anxiety-free life begins with awareness. Awareness is more than recognizing when anxiety strikes; it's about becoming attuned to the subtle signals your body sends when stress starts to take the reins – acknowledging the triggers, both obvious and subtle, and recognizing the patterns that contribute to the spiraling cycle of anxiety.

Consider your body as an intricate instrument, finely tuned to respond to the world around you. When you cultivate awareness, you start tuning in to the signals it sends. The tightness in your chest, the restlessness, the racing thoughts – these are not random occurrences but messages from your body, signaling a need for attention and care.

Understanding these signals requires a certain level of introspection. It's about creating a mental map of your emotional landscape, noting the valleys of calm and the peaks of tension. The beauty of this process lies in its simplicity – no need for complex psychological theories, just a genuine curiosity about your own inner workings.

Do Not Just Be Aware – Be Mindfully Aware

One of the most powerful tools in cultivating awareness is mindfulness. Rooted in ancient practices, mindfulness involves paying deliberate attention to the present moment without judgment. It's about observing your thoughts and feelings without getting entangled in them.

Mindfulness is not a magical solution that erases anxiety; rather, it's a lens through which you can view your experiences more objectively. When you cultivate mindfulness, you create a space between the stimulus and your response. In this space lies the power to choose how you react to stressors, a crucial element in the quest for an anxiety-free life.

The Anatomy of Worry

Worry is the distant cousin to anxiety. Like a persistent shadow, it often follows us through our daily life. To navigate the complex terrain of worry, we must first understand its anatomy—the intricate interplay of thoughts, emotions, and underlying fears that give rise to this seemingly relentless companion.

Unmasking the Thought Patterns

Catastrophic Thinking

At the heart of worry often lies catastrophic thinking—the tendency to anticipate the worst possible outcomes. Whether fueled by past experiences or an overactive imagination, catastrophic thinking magnifies the potential negatives, weaving a tapestry of anxiety.

Overgeneralization

Worriers often draw broad conclusions based on limited evidence. Overgeneralization involves taking a single negative event and projecting it onto all aspects of life. This cognitive distortion can amplify worry by creating a distorted perception of reality.

Perfectionism

The pursuit of perfection can be a breeding ground for worry. The fear of falling short of impossibly high standards fuels an ongoing cycle of concern about performance, appearance, or societal expectations.

Emotions as Messengers

Fear

Worry is intimately linked with fear. Whether it's the fear of the unknown, fear of failure, or fear of judgment, understanding the specific fears beneath your worry is crucial. Fear, when acknowledged, becomes a guide, pointing toward areas that require attention and compassion.

Uncertainty

Worry often thrives in the soil of uncertainty. The discomfort of not knowing can trigger a cascade of anxious thoughts. Learning to tolerate uncertainty and adopting a mindset of flexibility can serve as a powerful antidote to worry.

The Role of Control

Illusion of Control

Worriers often seek control as a means of mitigating anxiety. However, the illusion of control can backfire, leading to increased worry when situations prove uncontrollable. Acknowledging the limits of control becomes a cornerstone in managing worry effectively.

Letting Go of Control

Ironically, loosening the grip on control can be a transformative strategy. Embracing the idea that not everything can be controlled allows for a more adaptive response to the uncertainties of life.

Breaking the Worry Loop

Mindfulness and Present-Moment Awareness

Worry often thrives in the past or the future. Mindfulness, rooted in present-moment awareness, becomes a potent tool for breaking the worry loop. By grounding yourself in the now, you disrupt the patterns of anxious thought.

Cognitive Restructuring

Challenge and reframe worry-inducing thoughts through cognitive restructuring. Identify irrational beliefs, question their validity, and replace them with more balanced perspectives. This process gradually shifts the neural pathways associated with worry.

Cultivating Resilience

Acceptance

Acceptance is not passive resignation but an active acknowledgment of reality. Embracing the uncertainties of life and acknowledging that some things are beyond control fosters resilience in the face of worry.

Self-Compassion

Replace self-criticism with self-compassion. Understand that worry, in many instances, arises from a genuine desire to protect oneself. Treat yourself with the same kindness you would offer a friend facing similar concerns.

Seeking Professional Support

Worry, when pervasive and debilitating, may warrant professional support. Therapists skilled in cognitive-behavioral techniques can guide you in unraveling the layers of worry and equipping you with practical tools for managing anxious thoughts.

Understanding worry is not about eradicating it entirely but about developing a nuanced relationship with this facet of the human experience. By dissecting the anatomy of worry, we lay the groundwork for cultivating a mindset that embraces uncertainty, fosters resilience, and paves the way toward a more tranquil existence.

What's Next?

In this chapter, we've delved into the roots of anxiety, exploring what triggers this age-old response in our modern lives. We've looked at the difference between healthy stress and the chronic anxiety that can tip the scales into an overwhelming burden. The upcoming chapters will equip you with techniques and practical strategies to not only recognize anxiety but also build a robust toolkit to release its grip. We're keeping it straightforward, relatable, and most importantly, actionable.

Chapter 2: Dealing with Stress – the First Steps

Nab the Culprits

Before dealing with stress and anxiety itself let's first identify the major sources of stress in our daily life. Here they are in no particular order:

1. ***Bills***: when our finances are not in order, there is a high tendency for us to get on edge when the bills are due. This can even get worse when we begin to feel like we cannot lay our hands on certain things that are very important to us. It's often at this point that we begin to mount pressure on ourselves in order to meet up. Recognizing this early can help us manage our emotions at moments like this.

2. ***Work***: this can be another primary source of stressors in our life. And this is not just limited to work or business. It extends to other people we work with -

the ungrateful and ever-demanding boss, the nagging colleague, the business partner that's not committed to the business but always wants huge returns. The list is endless. These things can linger on and begin to affect our personal life.

3. ***Personal relationships***: even those very dear to us can be the ones who stress us out (of course most times unintentionally). From children who don't want to cooperate at all, to spouses who seem to be oblivious to our plights. It can even be friends who betray us or parents who want to control our lives without our consent. The list can go on.

4. ***Unrealistic expectations***: sometimes we expect too much from ourselves or from others and when these expectations are not met, we get worked up. This happens because we seem not to understand that we do not have control over everything – we do not have control over certain situations and we do not have control over other people's actions. Understanding the limits of our control can help us manage our expectations.

5. ***Health conditions***: this is not the least of our stressors but then we are always aware of this because of the pain and discomfort it brings to us. The caveat here is to pay more attention to our body and how we feel.
Now that we've Identified the Culprit What's Next?

Dealing With the Culprits

Let's discuss some practical ways to tackle this situation. Here are some ways I've found to be effective in handling some of the major causes of stress above:

1. ***Identify your priorities***: firstly you've got to get your priorities right. Identify the things that are most important to you and take care of them first; then every other thing can come later. This might mean that you have to spend less money on certain things in order to have more to spend on more important things. You may also have to change your job, your hobbies, your friends and maybe even your environment entirely.

2. ***Managing expectations***: it's true that people expect a lot from us but it's our job to manage those expectations properly. We do not have to live a life of obligation to anyone. It's your duty to set boundaries with people and say no when necessary. On the other side you also have to learn not to expect too much from other people. No one owes you anything and you have no control over other people's lives – period.

3. ***Separate work from personal life***: learn to work in the office and live at home. After work, learn to leave everything about work at the office while going back home. While going to work, leave home matters at home.

4. ***You cannot do everything***: learn to work with people both at home and office – share responsibilities, delegate tasks and hire other people to help you out.

Focus on the most important tasks and let other people help you. Don't spread yourself too thin.

5. ***Connect with the right people***: connecting with the right people can serve as a shield against stress and anxiety. So visit the therapist, talk to a friend, join a support group, have a lunch with someone who cares, volunteer to help other people. You may find out that one good connection can be an anchor that will change your story for good.

6. ***Relaxation techniques***: learning how to relax in moments of heat can go a long way in helping you ease-off. Mindful breathing, massage, journaling, diets – these can all help you in your fight against stress. We are going to explore some of these in the upcoming chapters.

In our next chapter, we'll delve into the powerful world of mindful breathing techniques, a practice rooted in ancient wisdom that can provide immediate relief in the face of anxiety.

So, let's embark on this journey together – understanding anxiety, embracing change, and reclaiming the peace that's rightfully yours.

Chapter 3: Mindful Breathing Techniques

In this chapter, we'll explore the profound impact of mindful breathing and unveil practical techniques to incorporate this transformative practice into your daily life.

In today's fast-paced world, we often overlook the simple act of breathing, letting it fade into the background of our busy minds. But if we consciously tune into our breath, allowing it to ebb and flow naturally, it can be a powerful tool to help us unwind and regain control when life feels overwhelming. Mindful breathing is like a stress-busting superhero. It grounds us in the now, cutting through the clutter of future worries and past regrets. As we sync with our breathing's gentle rhythm, our minds too find peace and stillness.

Ancient Roots of Mindful Breathing

To fully grasp the strength of mindful breathing, we must journey back to its roots. Integral to practices such as yoga and meditation, it has been a key element of spiritual and philosophical teachings for ages.

Yoga and the Dance of Breath

In yoga, mindful breathing goes by the name pranayama, which translates to breath control. Prana, often seen as the life force, is thought to flow with the breath. Yogis manipulate this force through breathing techniques, aiming for a balance of body, mind, and spirit.

Meditation and the Anchor of Breath

Buddhist traditions hold mindfulness, especially through breath awareness, as a vital aspect of meditation. The breath becomes a point of focus, a steady beacon for the mind to return to whenever it strays. This practice sharpens concentration and fosters profound self-awareness.

Why Mindful Breathing Works

Curious about how breathing can be a secret weapon against stress and anxiety? Here's the rundown:

1. *Soothing the Nervous System*

The Science: Engaging in mindful breathing activates the parasympathetic nervous system, our body's chill-out mode. It dials down the stress response, slowing our heartbeat and calming our bodily functions.

The Philosophy: In yogic thought, this calming effect is about balancing inner energies, symbolized by the sun and moon. Mindful breathing harmonizes these forces, leading to inner peace.

2. *Calming the Emotional Brain*

The Science: The amygdala, our emotional alarm bell, becomes less reactive to stress with regular mindful breathing. This means better emotional control and less anxiety.

The Philosophy: Mindfulness traditions use the breath as a mental anchor, helping us stay rooted in the present. This practice reduces the power of rampant emotions, echoing the Buddhist practice of 'sati' or mindfulness.

3. *Sharpening the Mind and Its Adaptability*

The Science: Mindful breathing can boost cognitive functions and the brain's adaptability. It's like mental armor against the wear and tear of stress.

The Philosophy: Meditation compares the mind to a sky filled with passing clouds of thoughts. Mindful breathing parts these clouds, allowing mental clarity. This is akin to the yogic state of 'Samadhi,' a deep, undisturbed focus.

Practical Techniques for Mindful Breathing

1. *Abdominal Breathing*
→ Get comfy sitting or lying down.
→ Place one hand on your chest, the other on your belly.
→ Breathe in deeply through your nose, feel your belly rise.
→ Breathe out slowly with pursed lips, belly falling.
→ Keep at it, focusing on the movement of your belly.

2. *The 4-7-8 Technique*
→ Sit up straight and relax.
→ Inhale quietly through the nose for four seconds.
→ Hold that breath for seven seconds.

> → Exhale completely through the mouth for eight seconds.
> → Keep repeating, building up as you get used to it.

3. Box Breathing
> → Inhale through the nose for four seconds.
> → Hold that breath for another four.
> → Exhale through the mouth for four seconds.
> → Pause for four seconds before the next breath.
> → Continue this pattern, keeping each part even.

How to Incorporate Mindful Breathing into Your Daily Life

1. *Morning Ritual*

Begin your day with a few minutes of mindful breathing. Set an intention for the day and let each breath infuse you with a sense of calm and focus.

2. *Micro-Mindfulness Breaks*

Throughout the day, take micro-mindfulness breaks. Pause for a few moments, close your eyes, and engage in a few mindful breaths. It's a reset button for the mind.

3. *Transition Moments*

Incorporate mindful breathing during transitional moments – before a meeting, while waiting in line, or during your commute. Use these moments as opportunities to center yourself.

4. *Evening Wind-Down*

As you wind down in the evening, use mindful breathing to release the tensions of the day. Let each breath signal a shift from activity to rest.

Cultivating a Mindful Lifestyle

As you embark on the journey of mindful breathing, consider it not as a standalone practice but as a gateway to a more mindful lifestyle. Each breath becomes a reminder – a moment to bring awareness to your thoughts, emotions, and actions.

In our next chapter, we'll unravel the layers of "The Art of Letting Go," a crucial element in the anxiety detox journey. So, continue to breathe mindfully, embrace the present moment, and savor the tranquility that unfolds within each breath.

Chapter 4: The Art of Letting Go

One of the chief reasons why people get stressed out is that they are either in a constant struggle with their past mistakes or they worry too much about the future. Understanding what's within your control and letting go of what's not within your control is key to effective stress management. In this chapter, we'll provide you with practical techniques to do this.

Understanding the Weight We Carry

Before we embark on the journey of letting go, it's crucial to acknowledge the weight we often carry – the baggage of past experiences, the anxieties about the future, and the expectations we place upon ourselves. These burdens, though invisible, can be incredibly heavy, creating a persistent undercurrent of stress in our lives.

How the Past and the Future Affect Us

Although we can sometimes draw strength and experiences from the past, we seem to mostly remember negative experiences from the past rather than the positive ones. This often leaves us with regrets, grudges, and unresolved emotions from these negative past experiences that can permeate our thoughts, casting shadows on our current moments.

Likewise, an obsession with the future – its uncertainties, potential failures, and the relentless pursuit of perfection – can sow the seeds of anxiety. The constant projection into what lies ahead distracts us from the richness of the present and amplifies the stress of the unknown.

The Essence of Letting Go

Release and Freedom

Letting go is not a dismissal of the past or a neglect of the future; it's a conscious act of release. It's about acknowledging the weight we carry, understanding its impact on our well-being, and choosing to set it down. In the act of letting go, we reclaim the present, freeing ourselves from the shackles of what was and what might be.

Living in the Present

At its core, letting go is an invitation to fully inhabit the present moment. It's an acknowledgment that the present is where life unfolds, where joy is found, and where we have the power to shape our experiences. By releasing the grip on the past and future – which we have no control over, we create space for serenity and authenticity in the now.

The Power of Forgiveness

At the heart of letting go is forgiveness – not just for others but, perhaps more importantly, for ourselves. Holding onto resentment, guilt, or anger binds us to the past, hindering our capacity to live fully in the present. Forgiveness is a profound act of self-love, a gift that unburdens the heart and opens the door to healing.

Practical Steps to Forgiveness

- Acknowledge Your Feelings: Understand and accept the emotions tied to past experiences. Recognition is the first step towards release.

- Empathy and Understanding: Try to see the situation from different perspectives, fostering empathy for yourself and others involved.
- Write a Letter: Consider writing a letter to express your feelings, whether you choose to send it or not. The act of writing can be therapeutic.
- Cultivate Compassion: Recognize that everyone, including yourself, is human and prone to mistakes. Cultivate compassion for the imperfections of life.

Change Happens Often

Anxiety may also stem from our resistance to change, our desire for permanence in an ever-evolving world. Letting go involves embracing the concept of impermanence – understanding that change is the only constant. When we accept the transitory nature of life, we open ourselves to the beauty of each moment without the fear of losing it.

Mindfulness in Accepting Change

Practicing mindfulness is a powerful tool in embracing impermanence. It involves observing each moment without attachment, recognizing that it arises, flourishes, and dissolves. In this awareness, we find a profound sense of freedom, unshackled from the grip of an unattainable permanence.

Practical Techniques for Letting Go

1. *Mindful Meditation*
Procedure
→ Find a quiet space and sit comfortably.
→ Focus on your breath, allowing thoughts to come and go without attachment.
→ When memories or worries arise, acknowledge them without judgment and guide your focus back to the present moment.
→ Gradually extend the duration of your meditation as you become more comfortable with letting go of fleeting thoughts.

2. *Release Rituals*
Procedure
→ Write down burdensome thoughts or emotions on paper.
→ In a safe environment, set the paper ablaze, symbolizing the release of these burdens.
→ Witness the flames and visualize the weight lifting as the paper turns to ash.

3. *Using Affirmations*
Procedure

→ Create positive affirmations that counteract self-limiting beliefs or anxieties.

→ Repeat these affirmations regularly, reinforcing a mindset of empowerment and self-love.

Letting go is not a one-time event; it's a continuous, evolving process. As we navigate the complexities of life, new challenges and opportunities for release will emerge. The art lies in cultivating a mindset that welcomes the ever-changing nature of existence.

Chapter 5: Eat Your Way out of Stress

The relationship between what we eat and our mental well-being is beyond what we can imagine. Healthy eating routine, as an integral part of stress management, recognizes the interconnectedness of our physical health and mental equilibrium. In this chapter, we'll delve into the foundations of holistic nutrition, understanding how the food we choose can influence our stress levels, and practical guidelines for embracing a nourishing and calming approach to nutrition.

The Mind-Body Connection

Food is not merely fuel for the body; it's a source of vital nutrients that play a crucial role in our mental and emotional states. The choices we make in our diet can either contribute to stress or act as a balm for the nervous system. Healthy eating can foster a balance that supports both physical and mental well-being.

Foods that help you beat Stress

1. *Complex Carbohydrates (Serotonin Boost)*

Complex carbohydrates, found in foods like whole grains, legumes, and vegetables, play a vital role in promoting serotonin production. Serotonin is a neurotransmitter known for its mood-regulating effects. Including a variety of complex carbohydrates in your diet provides a steady release of energy and contributes to a more stable mood.

2. *Omega-3 Fatty Acids (For Brain Health and Stress Reduction)*

Omega-3 fatty acids, abundant in fatty fish, flaxseeds, and walnuts, are essential for brain health. These fatty acids have been linked to reducing inflammation in the brain and promoting optimal functioning. Incorporating omega-3-rich foods supports cognitive function and helps mitigate the impact of stress on the brain.

3. *Magnesium (For Relaxation)*

Magnesium, found in leafy greens, nuts, seeds, and whole grains, is often referred to as the "relaxation mineral." It plays a crucial role in muscle function and relaxation. A diet rich in magnesium can contribute to a sense of calmness and help alleviate muscle tension associated with stress.

4. *Vitamin B Complex (For Balancing Stress Hormones)*

B vitamins, including B6, B12, and folate, are essential for the synthesis of neurotransmitters involved in mood regulation. A deficiency in these vitamins can impact stress resilience. Foods like lean meats, leafy greens, and legumes provide a spectrum of B vitamins crucial for maintaining mental well-being.

5. *Antioxidants (Cellular Protection)*

Antioxidants, abundant in colorful fruits and vegetables, combat oxidative stress – a contributor to chronic inflammation. By protecting cells from damage, antioxidants contribute to overall health and resilience against the physiological effects of stress.

Practical Tips for Everyday Nutrition

I'm excited to guide you on this journey towards better stress management through healthy eating routine because most times what we eat affect how we feel. It's not just about sustenance; it's about providing your body and mind with the right fuel. For stress management, we'll focus on incorporating foods that support a calm and resilient state.

Let's break it down to some actionable steps tailored to your needs.

1. ***Balanced and Varied Diet***: Strive for a well-rounded diet that incorporates a variety of nutrient-dense foods. Include a spectrum of colors in your fruits and vegetables to ensure a broad range of vitamins, minerals, and antioxidants.
2. ***Mindful Eating***: Take a moment with each meal. Notice the colors, savor the flavors, and be present in the experience. This mindful approach fosters a deeper connection between your mind and body.
3. ***Hydration***: Don't forget the power of water. Aim for at least 8 cups a day. Proper hydration supports overall wellness and keeps your body functioning optimally.
4. ***Limit Stimulants***: While a cup of coffee is okay, too much caffeine can contribute to jitteriness. Aim for

balance, and consider herbal teas for a calming alternative.

5. ***Sugar Moderation***: Opt for natural sweeteners like honey or maple syrup when needed. Minimize processed sugars, as they can lead to energy crashes.

Holistic nutrition transcends individual meals; it's a lifestyle that embraces the principles of balance, mindfulness, and respect for the body's inherent wisdom. As you integrate these practices into your daily life, you'll discover the transformative power of holistic nutrition for promoting calm and resilience.

Remember, this is a journey, not a destination. Gradual changes lead to lasting results. Feel free to experiment with these meal ideas and adjust based on your preferences. Let's nourish your body, calm your mind, and cultivate resilience together!

PS: *To make your journey smooth and easy, I have prepared a whole-week meal plan for you. You can find it attached in the appendix I of this book*

Why we get worried

Chapter 6: Journaling for Emotional Release

Journaling is another very important tool in your stress management arsenal. It helps you ease off certain burdens and sets you on the path to self-discovery. In this chapter, we'll uncover the therapeutic benefits of journaling, explore various techniques, and guide you on a journey of emotional release through the art of putting pen to paper.

The Power of the Pen

Journaling provides a sacred space where your thoughts, emotions, and innermost reflections can unfold without judgment. It acts as a confidant, allowing you to express the full spectrum of your feelings in a safe and private sanctuary. Through the act of writing, you embark on a journey of self-discovery, navigating the landscapes of your mind and heart.

Therapeutic Benefits of Journaling

Emotional Release

Writing down your thoughts and emotions can be cathartic. It's a way to release what's swirling within, offering a tangible outlet for the intangible weight we carry. Whether it's joy, frustration, sadness, or excitement, journaling provides a medium to acknowledge and let go.

Clarity and Self-Reflection

The process of putting thoughts into words brings clarity. As you articulate your feelings on paper, patterns and insights emerge. Journaling becomes a mirror reflecting your inner landscape, fostering a deeper understanding of yourself and the roots of your emotions.

Stress Reduction

The act of journaling helps declutter the mind. When thoughts are penned down, they cease to be elusive fragments, becoming tangible entities that can be explored and understood. This mental decluttering contributes to stress reduction, creating space for a more peaceful and focused mind.

Techniques for Effective Journaling

Stream of Consciousness Writing (Flowing Without Constraints)

Set a timer for 10-15 minutes and write without pausing or censoring. Allow your thoughts to flow freely, even if they seem disjointed. This technique taps into the subconscious, revealing hidden thoughts and emotions.

Gratitude Journaling (Focusing on the Positive)

Each day, jot down three things you're grateful for. This practice shifts your focus towards positivity, fostering a mindset of appreciation and resilience in the face of challenges.

Letter Writing (Unsent Letters of Release)

Write a letter to someone or something that has caused you distress. Pour out your feelings, grievances, and wishes, even if you never intend to send the letter. This exercise can be remarkably liberating.

Prompt-Based Journaling (Guiding Reflections)

Use prompts to guide your writing. For example:
"Today, I feel…"
"One thing I learned about myself is…"
"My response to stress is…"

Integrating Journaling into Your Routine

Morning Reflections

Set aside 10 minutes each morning to reflect on your feelings, goals for the day, and any concerns. This sets a positive tone for the day ahead.

Evening Unwind

Before bed, spend a few minutes processing the events of the day. Acknowledge your accomplishments, express gratitude, and release any lingering stress.

Creative Expression

If words don't suffice, incorporate drawings, doodles, or collages into your journal. Creative expression provides an alternative avenue for emotional release.

Embracing the Journey

Remember, your journal is a compass for your personal odyssey. There are no rules or judgments; it's a canvas for your authenticity. As you navigate the realms of emotions, let your pen be the guide, helping you release, reflect, and rediscover the resilience within.

Chapter 7: Nature Therapy for Stress Management

In the hustle and bustle of modern life, the healing embrace of nature offers a sanctuary for the mind, body, and soul. Nature therapy, also known as ecotherapy or green therapy, harnesses the revitalizing power of the natural world to alleviate stress and promote overall well-being. In this chapter, we'll explore the profound impact of nature therapy, its connection to stress management, and practical techniques to integrate the therapeutic benefits of nature into our lives.

The Healing Essence of Nature

Nature has an inherent ability to soothe, rejuvenate, and inspire. The rustling of leaves in the wind, the gentle flow of a stream, or the vibrant hues of a sunset create a symphony of serenity that resonates with our deepest selves. Understanding the therapeutic potential of nature involves recognizing the intricate connection between our well-being and the natural world.

The Connection Between Nature and Stress

The urban landscape, with its concrete structures and bustling pace, often contributes to the stressors we encounter. Nature therapy provides an antidote, offering an escape from the relentless demands of city life. The calming effect of natural surroundings has been shown to reduce cortisol levels, lower heart rate, and induce a state of relaxation.

Restoring Attention Fatigue

Constant exposure to screens, notifications, and the demands of modern work can lead to attention fatigue. Nature, with its inherently captivating yet gentle stimuli, helps restore attention. This phenomenon, known as attention restoration theory, suggests that exposure to nature allows the brain's attention resources to replenish, leading to improved focus and mental clarity.

The Therapeutic Benefits of Nature

Stress Reduction and Cortisol Regulation

Cortisol, often referred to as the stress hormone, plays a significant role in the body's fight-or-flight response. Spending time in nature has been linked to a reduction in cortisol levels, contributing to an overall sense of relaxation and stress relief.

Improved Mood and Emotional Well-Being

Nature therapy has a profound impact on mood and emotional well-being. Exposure to natural environments has been associated with decreased feelings of anxiety and depression. The beauty of nature has a unique ability to uplift the spirit, fostering a positive outlook on life.

Enhanced Creativity and Problem-Solving Skills

Nature therapy nurtures creativity. Time spent in natural settings has been shown to enhance creative thinking and problem-solving skills. The open and expansive nature of outdoor environments encourages innovative thought and a broader perspective.

Physical Health Benefits

Beyond mental well-being, nature therapy contributes to physical health. Spending time outdoors has been linked to improved immune function, reduced blood pressure, and a lower risk of various health conditions.

Practical Techniques for Nature Therapy

Forest Bathing (Shinrin-Yoku)
→ Find a quiet forested area.
→ Engage your senses – observe the colors, listen to the sounds, feel the textures.
→ Take slow, intentional breaths, immersing yourself in the forest atmosphere.
→ Allow yourself to be present, letting go of distractions and worries.

Nature Walks or Hikes
→ Explore local parks, trails, or natural reserves.
→ Set aside dedicated time for nature walks or hikes, allowing yourself to disconnect from electronic devices.
→ Notice the details – the rustling leaves, the bird songs, the play of sunlight through the trees.

Outdoor Meditation

→ Choose a quiet outdoor space.
→ Sit comfortably and focus on your breath.
→ Incorporate nature elements into your meditation – the warmth of the sun, the feel of the breeze.

→ Allow the sounds of nature to become part of your meditative experience.

Integrating Nature Therapy into Daily Life

Nature therapy is not reserved for special occasions; it can be seamlessly woven into our daily lives. As you embrace the therapeutic benefits of nature, consider these practices:

- Create a Nature Ritual: Dedicate a specific time each day or week for a nature ritual, whether it's a morning walk, an afternoon tour in a nearby park, or simply a moment of mindful observation in your backyard.
- Green Spaces at Home: If possible, cultivate green spaces at home. Whether it's a small garden, a balcony with potted plants, or even a windowsill adorned with flowers, having a touch of nature in your living space can contribute to your well-being.
- Mindful Observation: Develop the habit of mindful observation. Even in urban environments, take a few moments to notice the natural elements around you – a patch of sky, a tree-lined street, or a flower pushing through the pavement.

So, step outside, breathe in the fresh air, and let the therapeutic embrace of nature guide you towards stress relief and well-being.

Chapter 8: Energy Healing Techniques

In the realm of all-round well-being, energy healing techniques offer a profound exploration into the vital forces that underpin our physical, emotional, and mental states. This chapter invites you to embark on a journey into the world of energy healing—an ancient yet timeless practice that recognizes and works with the subtle energies that flow through and around us. Unveil the transformative potential of energy healing as we delve into various techniques that contribute to balance, restoration, and a harmonious integration of mind and body.

Understanding Energy Healing

Energy healing operates on the principle that subtle energies influence our health and well-being.

While these energies might be imperceptible to the naked eye, various traditions and practices have acknowledged their existence for centuries. This chapter explores how energy healing techniques tap into these subtle forces, aiming to bring about a state of balance and vitality.

Common Energy Healing Techniques

We're going to explore some of the core energy healing practices but it's practically impossible to fully teach you how to use these techniques here. To enjoy the benefits of these practices, you can search for video guides on the YouTube or seek out professional support

1. Reiki Healing

Reiki, a Japanese practice, involves the gentle laying of hands on or near the body to channel universal life energy. This technique aims to balance and harmonize the body's energy centers, promoting relaxation and facilitating the body's natural healing abilities.

2. Acupuncture and Acupressure

Rooted in Traditional Chinese Medicine, acupuncture and acupressure involve stimulating specific points along the body's meridians. By doing so, these techniques aim to regulate the flow of energy, known as Qi, addressing imbalances and promoting overall well-being.

3. Crystal Healing

Crystal healing involves placing crystals on or around the body to balance and direct energy. Each crystal is believed to possess unique properties that influence energy flow. This technique is often used to cleanse, energize, and harmonize the energy centers.

4. Chakra Balancing

Chakras, energy centers aligned along the spine, play a crucial role in many energy healing practices. Techniques such as meditation, visualization, and the use of specific stones aim to balance and align the chakras, promoting a sense of equilibrium.

5. Qi Gong

Qi Gong, a Chinese practice, combines movement, breath, and meditation to cultivate and balance Qi, the vital life force. Through slow, intentional movements, practitioners seek to harmonize the body's energy, promoting overall health and well-being.

Integrating Energy Healing into Your Life

1. Personal Energy Awareness

Begin by cultivating awareness of your own energy. Regularly check in with yourself, paying attention to sensations, emotions, and areas of tension. This self-awareness lays the foundation for understanding and influencing your energetic state.

2. Seek Professional Guidance

Consider working with experienced energy healers who can provide personalized sessions based on your unique needs. Whether through Reiki, acupuncture, or other modalities, professional guidance can deepen your exploration of energy healing.

3. Daily Practices for Balance

Integrate energy-balancing practices into your daily routine. This might include a few minutes of focused breathing, meditation, or using crystals. Consistent daily rituals contribute to the maintenance of a balanced energy state.

The Journey of Energy Healing

As you explore energy healing techniques, recognize that this journey is deeply personal. Each individual may resonate with different practices, and the key lies in discovering what aligns with your unique energy blueprint. By delving into these ancient and transformative techniques, you open the door to a realm where the subtle forces within and around you contribute to a profound sense of well-being.

Chapter 9: The Art and Science of Massage Therapy

Massage is not just a physical experience; it's an art form that weaves together touch, intention, and presence. Imagine it as a harmonious dance that aligns your body, mind, and spirit. The hands of a skilled massage therapist are not merely delivering strokes—they are conduits of healing, tapping into your body's innate ability to release tension, restore balance, and usher in a profound sense of relaxation.

How a Massage Session Can help you with Stress

1. Stress Reduction

The gentle kneading and soothing strokes of a massage are a balm for the nervous system. As tension melts away, the body enters a state of relaxation, triggering the release of endorphins—the body's natural stress relievers.

2. Muscle Relaxation and Pain Relief

Targeted manipulation of muscles alleviates tightness and reduces pain. Whether it's the result of daily stress, poor posture, or physical exertion, massage helps soothe muscular discomfort, fostering a renewed sense of ease.

3. Improved Circulation

Massage enhances blood circulation, promoting the efficient delivery of oxygen and nutrients to cells throughout the body. This heightened circulation supports overall health and aids in the removal of metabolic waste, contributing to a revitalized system.

4. Enhanced Flexibility and Joint Mobility

The stretching and manipulation involved in certain massage techniques improve joint flexibility and range of motion. This is particularly beneficial for individuals dealing with stiffness or those seeking to enhance athletic performance.

5. Mental Clarity and Focus

Beyond the physical realm, massage has a profound impact on mental well-being. The calming effect of massage aids in reducing mental chatter, promoting mental clarity, and fostering a heightened sense of focus.

6. Emotional Release and Well-Being

Touch is a powerful communicator of emotions. Massage provides a safe space for emotional release, allowing suppressed feelings to surface and dissipate. This emotional catharsis contributes to a sense of well-being and balance.

Choose the Right Type of Massage for You

1. Swedish Massage

Swedish massage, often considered a classic, involves long, flowing strokes that vary in pressure. This technique promotes relaxation, eases muscle tension, and improves circulation. It serves as an excellent introduction to the world of massage.

2. Deep Tissue Massage

For those seeking more intense relief, deep tissue massage penetrates into the underlying layers of muscle and connective tissue. It's effective in addressing chronic muscular issues and promoting recovery from injuries.

3. Shiatsu Massage

Rooted in traditional Japanese medicine, Shiatsu involves applying pressure to specific points along the body's meridians. This technique aims to balance the body's energy flow, promoting relaxation and overall well-being.

4. Thai Massage

Thai massage combines acupressure with assisted yoga stretches. Therapists use their hands, knees, legs, and feet to guide the recipient through a series of yoga-like poses. This dynamic technique enhances flexibility and promotes energy flow.

5. Aromatherapy Massage

Aromatherapy massage combines the benefits of massage with the therapeutic properties of essential oils. The chosen oils not only add a delightful fragrance but also contribute to specific therapeutic effects, such as relaxation or invigoration.

6. Hot Stone Massage

Hot stone massage involves placing heated stones on specific points of the body and using them as tools to massage. The warmth enhances muscle relaxation and allows for deeper penetration of therapeutic effects.

Setting the Scene for the Massage Experience

1. Communication and Trust

The foundation of a transformative massage experience lies in open communication between the client and the therapist. Clearly express your preferences, any specific concerns, and your desired outcome. Establishing trust creates a safe space for relaxation and healing.

2. Environment and Ambiance

The setting plays a pivotal role in the efficacy of a massage. Create an ambiance that fosters tranquility—soft lighting, calming music, and a comfortable temperature contribute to a nurturing environment.

3. Breath Awareness

Focus on your breath during the massage. Deep, mindful breathing enhances relaxation, facilitates the release of tension, and promotes a meditative state.

4. Post-Massage Care

Hydrate after a massage to help flush out released toxins. Take some time to rest and allow the benefits of the massage to fully integrate into your system. Gentle stretches can further enhance the positive effects.

The Journey Continues

As we conclude this chapter on massage therapy, remember that the benefits extend beyond the massage table. It's a journey of self-care, a commitment to honoring your body and mind. Whether you choose the soothing strokes of Swedish massage or the targeted relief of deep tissue techniques, each session becomes a chapter in your personal narrative of well-being.

Allow the healing touch of massage to be a melody that accompanies you through the symphony of life, promoting relaxation, restoring balance, and nurturing the essence of your being.

Chapter 10: Destroy Stress – Not Your Life

In a bid to deal with stress, it's not uncommon for us to turn to activities that, unknowingly, pose risks to our well-being. Influenced by friends, media, or various sources, we might consider options like excessive drinking, smoking, or experimenting with substances, thinking they offer a quick remedy for stress. However, the reality is that these shortcuts can lead to severe consequences in the long haul.

The Hidden Dangers

1. Excessive Drinking: What may start as a way to unwind can easily escalate into a habit that affects not only your mental health but your physical well-being.

Excessive alcohol consumption can lead to dependency, liver damage, and a myriad of health issues.

2. Smoking: The allure of a quick stress-relief puff can turn into a lifelong struggle with addiction. Smoking not only jeopardizes your respiratory health but also increases the risk of heart disease and various cancers.

3. Substance Ingestion: Experimentation with substances might seem like an escape, but it often leads to a path of dependency, impaired cognitive function, and a host of other health and social problems.

The Long-Term Impact

Quick fixes rarely provide lasting solutions, and in the realm of stress management, they can exacerbate the very issues we aim to resolve. These activities not only compromise our physical health but also impact our mental and emotional well-being. As the initial relief wears off, stress returns, often accompanied by new challenges stemming from these risky behaviors.

Building Resilience Instead

Rather than resorting to potentially harmful practices, consider channeling your energy into constructive and resilient strategies to combat stress:

1. Mindfulness Practices: Engage in mindfulness meditation or yoga to cultivate awareness and calm the mind. These practices build resilience and provide lasting stress-relief.

2. Healthy Lifestyle Choices: Regular exercise, a balanced diet, and sufficient sleep are powerful tools in stress management. They contribute not only to physical health but also enhance mental and emotional well-being.

3. Professional Support: If stress becomes overwhelming, seeking guidance from a mental health professional can provide effective coping mechanisms and a supportive space to navigate challenges.

Your Well-Being Matters

Remember, your well-being is paramount. Destructive habits may seem like a shortcut, but they often lead to longer and more challenging detours. By choosing resilience over risky practices, you're investing in a future where stress doesn't dictate your life but becomes a manageable part of it.

As we conclude this journey through stress management, let it be a reminder that destroying stress is about building a life that thrives despite its presence. It's about choosing paths that lead to lasting well-being rather than fleeting escapes.

May your journey toward a stress-resilient life be filled with self-care, positive choices, and the strength to face challenges with resilience.

Take care,
Jose

You are Invited

Dear Valued Reader,

Congratulations on completing the journey through this book: "Why We Get Worried: A Practical Guide to Letting Go of Worry and Anxiety and Living A Stress-Free Life." Your commitment to self-improvement and well-being is commendable.

As you close the book, I want to express my heartfelt appreciation for allowing these insights to become a part of your life. I hope you found practical strategies that resonate with your journey toward a stress-free, joy-filled existence.

Here's my invitation to share your thoughts

If the book made a positive impact on you, could you share your thoughts in a review? Your feedback helps others, and it inspires me to keep creating helpful stuff.

Your experience matters, and your review can help others too.

Thank you for being an integral part of this transformative journey. Wishing you a life filled with resilience, happiness, and the strength to embrace every moment.

Keep rocking,

Jose Andrews

Unleash Your Energy Potential!

Here's one last invitation from me

Once again congratulations on completing "Why We Get Worried"!

What if I told you there's a key to unlocking boundless energy and banishing fatigue?

Allow me to introduce you to my powerhouse guide, "WHY WE GET TIRED."

Inside, you'll discover the secret thieves stealing your energy unbeknownst to you.

This book will also expose you to 20 game-changing ways to reclaim your vitality and elevate your life. Master the top 3 methods to swiftly recharge your energy when it hits rock bottom.

This book is a no-nonsense powerhouse—short, concise, and straight to the point. Say goodbye to fluff and hello to a vibrant, energized YOU!

Ready to break free from tiredness and welcome boundless energy?

Grab your copy now and embark on the journey to an unstoppable, energy-filled life.

Here's Your Access Link

Or

You can just scan the code below

Don't miss out—your energy revolution starts here!

Energized regards,

Jose Andrews

Appendix I

Here's Your 7-Day Meal Plan for Stress Management

Day 1: Serotonin-Boosting Start

Breakfast: Serotonin-Boosting Smoothie
  - *Ingredients:*
    - 1 banana
    - 1 cup berries
    - 1 tablespoon flaxseeds
    - 1/2 cup Greek yogurt
    - Handful of spinach
    - Splash of almond milk

- *Instructions*:
- Blend all ingredients until smooth.

Lunch: Omega-3 Power Salad
  - *Ingredients:*
    - Grilled salmon or tofu
    - Quinoa
    - Mixed greens
    - Avocado
    - Cherry tomatoes

- *Instructions*:

- Assemble the ingredients in a bowl, drizzle with olive oil, and enjoy!

Snack: Nutrient-Packed Trail Mix

- *Ingredients:*
  - Almonds
  - Walnuts
  - Dark chocolate
  - Dried blueberries

- *Instructions*:

- Mix in a bowl and portion out for a convenient, stress-busting snack.

Dinner: Balanced Veggie Stir-Fry

- *Ingredients:*
  - Tofu or chicken
  - Brown rice
  - Broccoli, bell peppers, and snap peas
  - Sesame oil and soy sauce

- *Instructions*:

- Stir-fry your protein and veggies, then toss with cooked brown rice.

Day 2: Nourishing Breakfast Bowl

Breakfast: Nourishing Breakfast Bowl
- *Ingredients:*
  - Overnight oats
  - Sliced banana
  - Chia seeds
  - Greek yogurt
  - Drizzle of honey

- *Instructions*:
  - Mix ingredients in a bowl the night before and refrigerate. Top with sliced banana and a drizzle of honey in the morning.

Lunch: Quinoa and Chickpea Salad
- *Ingredients:*
  - Quinoa
  - Chickpeas
  - Cucumber, cherry tomatoes, red onion
  - Feta cheese
  - Olive oil and lemon dressing

- *Instructions*:
  - Combine all ingredients in a bowl and toss with olive oil and lemon dressing.

Snack: Apple Slices with Nut Butter
  - *Ingredients:*
    - Apple slices
    - Almond or peanut butter

  - *Instructions*:
  - Spread nut butter on apple slices for a satisfying and nutritious snack.

Dinner: Baked Salmon with Sweet Potato
  - *Ingredients:*
    - Baked salmon fillet
    - Roasted sweet potatoes
    - Steamed broccoli
    - Lemon and herb seasoning

  - *Instructions*:
  - Season salmon with herbs, bake, and serve with roasted sweet potatoes and steamed broccoli.

Day 3: Energizing Morning Smoothie

Breakfast: Energizing Morning Smoothie
  - *Ingredients:*
    - Spinach
    - Frozen mango chunks
    - Chia seeds
    - Coconut water

- *Instructions*:

- Blend ingredients until smooth for a refreshing and nutrient-packed start.

Lunch: Lentil and Vegetable Soup

- *Ingredients:*
  - Lentils
  - Carrots, celery, onions
  - Vegetable broth
  - Fresh herbs

- *Instructions*:

- Simmer lentils and vegetables in vegetable broth with fresh herbs for a comforting soup.

Snack: Greek Yogurt Parfait

- *Ingredients:*
  - Greek yogurt
  - Granola
  - Mixed berries

- *Instructions*:

- Layer Greek yogurt, granola, and mixed berries for a delightful and filling snack.

Dinner: Grilled Chicken Salad

- *Ingredients:*
  - Grilled chicken breast

- Romaine lettuce, cherry tomatoes, cucumber
- Avocado
- Balsamic vinaigrette dressing

- Instructions:

- Grill chicken and toss with fresh vegetables. Drizzle with balsamic vinaigrette dressing.

Day 4: Wholesome Breakfast Muffins

Breakfast: Wholesome Breakfast Muffins
- Ingredients:
- Whole-grain flour
- Grated carrots and zucchini
- Walnuts
- Greek yogurt
- Maple syrup

- Instructions:

- Bake muffins with whole-grain flour, grated carrots, zucchini, walnuts, and sweetened with a touch of maple syrup.

Lunch: Quinoa Stuffed Peppers
- Ingredients:
- Quinoa
- Bell peppers
- Black beans, corn, diced tomatoes

- Mexican seasoning

- Instructions:

- Stuff bell peppers with a mixture of quinoa, black beans, corn, and diced tomatoes seasoned with Mexican spices.

Snack: Trail Mix with Edamame
- Ingredients:

- Edamame
- Almonds
- Dried cranberries
- Dark chocolate

- Instructions:

- Combine edamame, almonds, dried cranberries, and dark chocolate for a protein-packed trail mix.

Dinner: Shrimp and Vegetable Stir-Fry
- Ingredients:

- Shrimp
- Broccoli, snow peas, carrots
- Brown rice
- Soy sauce and ginger

- Instructions:

- Stir-fry shrimp and vegetables, then toss with cooked brown rice. Season with soy sauce and ginger.

Day 5: Berry Bliss Breakfast Bowl

Breakfast: Berry Bliss Breakfast Bowl
- *Ingredients:*
  - Acai or mixed berry smoothie bowl
  - Granola
  - Sliced strawberries and kiwi
  - Drizzle of honey

- *Instructions*:
  - Blend acai or mixed berry smoothie bowl, top with granola, sliced strawberries, kiwi, and a drizzle of honey.

Lunch: Mediterranean Chickpea Salad
- *Ingredients:*
  - Chickpeas
  - Cherry tomatoes, cucumber, red onion
  - Feta cheese
  - Kalamata olives
  - Olive oil and lemon dressing

- *Instructions*:
  - Combine chickpeas, cherry tomatoes, cucumber, red onion, feta cheese, and Kalamata olives. Drizzle with olive oil and lemon dressing.

Snack: Avocado and Whole-Grain Crackers
- *Ingredients:*
  - Sliced avocado
  - Whole-grain crackers

- *Instructions*:
  - Enjoy sliced avocado with whole-grain crackers for a satisfying and nutrient-rich snack.

Dinner: Vegetable and Tofu Curry
- *Ingredients:*
  - Tofu
  - Mixed vegetables (bell peppers, zucchini, carrots)
  - Coconut milk
  - Curry spices

- *Instructions*:
  - Cook tofu and mixed vegetables in coconut milk with curry spices for a flavorful and nourishing curry.

Day 6: Green Goodness Smoothie

Breakfast: Green Goodness Smoothie
- *Ingredients:*
  - Kale or spinach
  - Pineapple chunks
  - Banana
  - Chia seeds

- Coconut water

- *Instructions*:

- Blend kale or spinach with pineapple chunks, banana, chia seeds, and coconut water for a nutrient-packed green smoothie.

Lunch: Brown Rice and Black Bean Bowl

- *Ingredients:*
  - Brown rice
  - Black beans
  - Corn, diced tomatoes, red onion
  - Avocado

- *Instructions*:

- Create a bowl with brown rice, black beans, corn, diced tomatoes, and topped with sliced avocado.

Snack: Yogurt-Dipped Strawberries

- *Ingredients:*
  - Greek yogurt
  - Fresh strawberries

- *Instructions*:

- Dip fresh strawberries in Greek yogurt for a delightful and protein-rich snack.

Dinner: Lemon Herb Baked Cod with Quinoa
- *Ingredients:*
  - Cod fillet
  - Lemon and herb seasoning
  - Quinoa
  - Steamed asparagus

- *Instructions*:

- Season cod fillet with lemon and herb seasoning, bake, and serve with quinoa and steamed asparagus.

Day 7: Hearty Breakfast Burrito

Breakfast: Hearty Breakfast Burrito
- *Ingredients:*
  - Whole-grain tortilla
  - Scrambled eggs or tofu
  - Black beans
  - Salsa and avocado

- *Instructions*:

- Fill a whole-grain tortilla with scrambled eggs or tofu, black beans, salsa, and sliced avocado for a hearty breakfast burrito.

Lunch: Spinach and Strawberry Salad
- *Ingredients:*
  - Spinach

- Sliced strawberries
- Goat cheese
- Walnuts
- Balsamic vinaigrette dressing

- Instructions:

- Toss spinach with sliced strawberries, goat cheese, walnuts, and drizzle with balsamic vinaigrette dressing.

Snack: Cottage Cheese with Pineapple

- Ingredients:

- Cottage cheese
- Fresh pineapple chunks

- Instructions:

- Enjoy a refreshing and protein-rich snack with cottage cheese and fresh pineapple chunks.

Dinner: Turkey and Vegetable Stir-Fry with Brown Rice

- Ingredients:

- Ground turkey
- Mixed vegetables (bell peppers, broccoli, carrots)
- Brown rice
- Soy sauce and ginger

- Instructions:

- Stir-fry ground turkey and mixed vegetables, then toss with cooked brown rice. Season with soy sauce and ginger.

Feel free to adjust portion sizes and ingredients based on your preferences and dietary needs. Remember, the key is variety, balance, and enjoying the nourishing journey.

If you have any specific dietary restrictions or preferences, be sure to consult with your doctor before using this meal plan. Cheers to a week of delicious and stress-relieving meals!

Appendix II

Chapter 1:

Anxiety and Depression Association of America (ADAA):

Website: https://adaa.org/

Statistic on anxiety disorders being the most common mental illness in the U.S.: https://adaa.org/

Fight-or-Flight Response:

Harvard Health Publishing:
https://www.health.harvard.edu/topics/stress

Mayo Clinic:
https://www.psychologytools.com/resource/fight-or-flight-response/

Chronic Anxiety:

National Institute of Mental Health:
https://www.nimh.nih.gov/health/topics/anxiety-disorders

American Psychological Association:
https://www.apa.org/topics/stress

Additional Resources:

National Alliance on Mental Illness (NAMI):
https://www.nami.org/Home

MentalHealth.gov: https://www.samhsa.gov/mental-health

The Jed Foundation: https://jedfoundation.org/

Chapter 3:

Scientific Research:

Harvard Health Publishing: https://www.health.harvard.edu/mind-and-mood/meditation-for-your-health

National Center for Complementary and Integrative Health: https://files.nccih.nih.gov/s3fs-public/Meditation_04-25-2016.pdf

American Psychological Association: https://westcoastrecoverycenters.com/what-are-mindfulness-based-interventions/

Books:

"Mindfulness in Plain English" by Bhante Gunaratana

"Wherever You Go, There You Are" by Jon Kabat-Zinn

"Breath: The New Science of Our Most Fundamental Act" by James Nestor

Websites and Apps:

Headspace: https://www.headspace.com/

Calm: https://www.calm.com/

UCLA Mindful Awareness Research Center: https://www.uclahealth.org/programs/marc

Chapter 4:

Books:

The Power of Now by Eckhart Tolle

The Untethered Soul by Michael A. Singer

The Courage to Be Vulnerable by Brené Brown

The Gifts of Imperfection by Brené Brown

Radical Forgiveness by Colin Tipping

The Forgiveness Project by Karen Armstrong

Additional Resources:

The Gottman Institute: https://www.gottman.com/ (Provides resources on stress management and healthy relationships)

Chapter 5:

Stress-Reducing Meal Plans and Recipes:

"The Mindful Diet" by Susan Peirce Thompson

"The Food Mood Connection" by Uma Naidoo

"The Anti-Stress Diet" by Dale Mathers

Websites:

https://www.mindbodygreen.com/

https://www.forksoverknives.com/

https://www.budgetbytes.com/

Additional Resources:

Academy of Nutrition and Dietetics:
https://www.eatright.org/

National Institute of Mental Health:
https://www.nimh.nih.gov/health/topics/anxiety-disord
ers

The American Institute of Stress:
https://www.stress.org/

Chapter 6:

JAMA Internal Medicine:
https://www.ncbi.nlm.nih.gov/pmc/articles/PMC66765
35/

The Greater Good Science Center:
https://greatergood.berkeley.edu/article/

Psychology Today:
https://www.psychologytoday.com/us/blog/the-creativ
e-life/201906/20-journal-prompts

Digital Journaling Options:

Day One: https://dayoneapp.com/

Journey:
https://help.journey.cloud/en/article/what-is-journey-1
cmxhui/

Penzu:
https://penzu.com/mobile/mobile_application/splash

Overcoming Obstacles:

Tiny Buddha:
https://tinybuddha.com/blog/5-ways-journaling-can-hel
p-you-get-through-the-hard-stuff/

Why we get worried

Psych Central:
https://medium.com/age-of-awareness/the-mental-blocks-keeping-you-away-from-journaling-2d264317afa9

Chapter 7:

American Psychological Association:
https://www.apa.org/topics/stress

National Health Service (UK):
https://www.nhshighland.scot.nhs.uk/health-and-wellbeing/feeling-good-outdoors/

Technology Integration:

NatureSpace:
https://apps.apple.com/us/app/naturespace-relax-sleep-dream/id312618509

SimplyWalk:
https://simply-walking-gps-map-steps.en.softonic.com/android

RelaxMelodies:
https://apps.apple.com/us/app/relax-melodies-sleep-sounds/id467103113?mt=12

Connecting with Nature:

Project Green Challenge:

https://projectgreenchallenge.com/

Chapter 8:

Scientific Basis:

Center for Reiki Research:

https://centerforreikiresearch.com/

Safety and Potential Risks:

Mayo Clinic:

https://www.mayoclinic.org/tests-procedures/acupuncture/about/risks/cmc-20392759

Alternative Options:

Progressive Muscle Relaxation Exercises:

https://www.anxietycanada.com/articles/how-to-do-progressive-muscle-relaxation/

Chapter 9:

American Massage Therapy Association:

https://www.amtamassage.org/

Massage Magazine: https://www.massagemag.com/

Thai Yoga Massage School of Austin:

https://theyogastudio.us/learn-thai-massage.html

www.ingramcontent.com/pod-product-compliance
Lightning Source LLC
Chambersburg PA
CBHW050830260726

48660CB00006B/2156